Original title:
A Universe of Laughs

Copyright © 2025 Creative Arts Management OÜ
All rights reserved.

Author: Nathaniel Blackwood
ISBN HARDBACK: 978-1-80567-864-9
ISBN PAPERBACK: 978-1-80567-985-1

Jokes in the Milky Way

Starships glide through cosmic glee,
Galactic puns are wild and free.
Black holes laugh with gravity,
While planets dance in jubilee.

A comet slips on space debris,
Winks at moons, quite cheekily.
Asteroids chuckle in their flight,
As space dust sparkles in the light.

Quips from the Quasar

Light-years away, the humor beams,
Quasars share their wittiest dreams.
They twinkle jokes across the void,
In laughter's echo, joy's employed.

Neutron stars, they spin and spin,
Telling tales where giggles begin.
Galaxies swirl, a comic dance,
In every chuckle, a cosmic chance.

The Comet's Comedic Tale

A comet zipped on its wild quest,
With jokes that sparked from east to west.
It tickled suns with fiery flair,
And made the moons giggle in air.

Through icy trails of mirth it flew,
With every tail, more laughter grew.
A cosmic prankster, swift it soared,
Leaving smiles, never bored.

Celestial Comedy Club

In an orbit, laughter takes the stage,
Where starlit comedians engage.
Nebulae burst with colorful sights,
As meteors share their funniest bites.

Planetary puns make comets roar,
With each punchline, the crowd wants more.
In this club of space and cheer,
Cosmic humor draws us near.

Glee Beyond the Galaxies

A comet with a silly grin,
Zooms past, like it's late for a spin.
Stars twinkle with jest and cheer,
Winking to all who wander near.

Planets bounce in a cosmic dance,
Each one dressed in a sparkly pants.
Moons giggle as they skip around,
While stardust tickles the ground.

Asteroids play tag in the night,
Dodging space rocks, what a sight!
Black holes puff with a hearty laugh,
As if they've found the perfect path.

Galaxies spiral in a jest,
Spreading joy, it's simply the best.
With echoes of mirth amid the light,
Who knew space could be such a delight?

Jovial Journeys Through Space

A rocket ship made of candy bars,
Zooms happily past the twinkling stars.
Bubbles rise in a fizzy spree,
As aliens sip celestial tea.

Nebulas twirl in polka-dot coats,
While laughter floats on fluffy boats.
Cosmic critters play leapfrog high,
Chasing their tails as they zip by.

Silly satellites pose for a snap,
Wobbling about in a giggly clap.
Every quasar sends a cheeky grin,
Inviting all to join in the din.

Across the cosmos, joy takes flight,
In the delightful dance of the night.
With each burst of laughter out far and wide,
In this playful galaxy, we all glide!

Infinite Amusement Above

Stars twinkle with glee, so bright,
Planets spin in a silly flight.
Comets dance like clowns on stage,
In this cosmic, playful age.

Galaxies swirl in a funky groove,
Nebulas laugh as they softly move.
Asteroids prank in a cheeky style,
Creating joy across every mile.

The Starlight Snicker.

In the cosmos, jokes unfold,
With whispers of humor, so bold.
Shooting stars make wishes fun,
As moons giggle in a playful run.

Black holes snicker, pulling us near,
Winking comets spark laughter, dear.
Each twinkle's a wink, a cheeky tease,
In the vastness where smiles never freeze.

Cosmic Giggles

Whirling rockets play hide and seek,
With the Milky Way's chuckle, unique.
And every pulsar beams with delight,
As they pulse out their laughs in the night.

Quasars shine with a vibrant flair,
Spreading joy through the cosmic air.
Unload your worries, just take a ride,
In this space where mirth can't hide.

Starlight Chuckles

Planets tease with a playful grin,
While meteor showers tickle the skin.
Solar winds carry giggles and cheer,
Filling the void with laughter near.

Astro cats pounce on beams of light,
Dancing around in the velvet night.
Every star shines with comical ways,
In this cosmic carnival that sways.

Laughing at Light Years

Stars twinkle like they know a joke,
Galaxies giggle as they spin and poke.
Planets dance in their orbits tight,
Winking at comets that zoom past in flight.

Gravity's pull can't weigh down the jest,
Black holes chuckle, they know they're the best.
In this vast space where humor's found,
Laughter echoes, a cosmic sound.

Cosmic Glee

Asteroids tumble with a clumsy cheer,
While space-time bends, causing all to leer.
Nebulas puff out in colorful play,
Spreading delight in a stellar ballet.

Each supernova bursts in a fit of giggles,
As stardust floats down, like tiny wiggles.
Planets collide, what a silly sight,
Making us chuckle, bringing pure delight.

The Solar Smirk

The sun beams brightly with a cheeky grin,
Behind every flare hides mischief within.
Mercury teases, racing on by,
While Venus rolls eyes with a cosmic sigh.

A solar wink causes a bright flare,
Jupiter's storms send giggles through air.
Rings of Saturn spin in joyful loops,
In this playful realm of celestial troops.

Synchronized Snickers

Moons chuckle softly in their tight-knit crew,
In synchronized dances, they laugh at the view.
Earth spins along, with a wobble and shake,
Creating a rhythm for laughter's sake.

Meteor showers bring whispers of fun,
As they dash through the night, one by one.
Every blink in the sky, a wink exchanged,
In this merry cosmos, forever arranged.

Witty Wanderlust

In a world where giggles fly,
Ticklish stars wink from the sky.
Socks on hands, shoes on heads,
Every step a laugh, no dread.

Bouncing rocks, a silly dance,
Around the sun, we take a chance.
Chasing joy like fireflies,
With every stumble, no goodbyes.

Laughter break, a cosmic spark,
Making friends with quips so stark.
The universe hums a cheeky tune,
Joyful echoes with every moon.

Laughter in the Dark Matter

In the shadows where we creep,
Funny creatures, no time to sleep.
Moonbeams giggle, they can't refrain,
Tickling stars in a galactic chain.

Every comet, a cheeky jest,
Whirling truths in cosmic quests.
Laughter ignites in the vast unknown,
Crafting smiles from the stars we've sown.

Whispers of wit float through space,
In the dark, we find our place.
With every twist, the cosmos plays,
In this dance of light, we graze.

The Comedy Constellation

Stars align in a wacky show,
Each twinkle bursting, ready to glow.
Jokers dressed in stellar guise,
Bringing joy and surprise.

Planets spin with comic grace,
A mirthful chase throughout the space.
Galaxies laugh, their colors swirl,
As laughter ripples and unfurls.

Meteors fly, a punchline course,
Splashing humor with great force.
In the great expanse, we find delight,
Chasing fun through the endless night.

Jovial Echoes

A cosmic cheer, a bright refrain,
Laughter ripples through the grain.
Milky way jokes, so sly, so clear,
Each tiny chuckle, we hold dear.

Silly thoughts, in stardust blend,
Time is funny, loops around the bend.
Every echo bounces back around,
Joyful sounds that make us abound.

Dancing comets, a merry chase,
In the void, we find a place.
With hearts so light, we play and spin,
In the laughter, we all win.

Starry Sillyness

In the sky where giggles twirl,
Stars play tag and dance and swirl.
Comets chuckle, zooming by,
While asteroids wink and say hi.

Nebulas puff up their cheeks,
Spitting out laughs and funny peaks.
Planets bounce in playful cheer,
Their merry tunes we all can hear.

Galactic Grins

In the void where the laughter soars,
Space critters jam on cosmic floors.
Jupiter jokes with Saturn's rings,
While Martians teach us how to sing.

Through black holes, the humor flows,
Tickling stars with funny prose.
Quasars blush in shades of glee,
As they watch the cosmic spree.

Moonbeam Mirth

Under moonlight, shadows prance,
With twinkling eyes, they join the dance.
Whimsical whispers fill the air,
While giggly craters spread their flair.

On lunar paths, the jokes align,
As stardust spreads the punchline.
Winking beams share playful sights,
Turning darkness into laughs so bright.

Comedic Constellations

Orion tells tales of silly fights,
While Pegasus flaps, soaring heights.
Ursa Major rolls with glee,
As Cassiopeia laughs heartily.

Stars conspire with cheeky play,
Showing laughter in their sway.
Together they form a jolly crew,
In the sky, where joy shines through.

Bouncing Across Lightyears

Stars twinkle like playful sprites,
In the night, they dance and bite.
Galaxies spin with giggles bright,
As comets race in sheer delight.

Asteroids chuckle as they roam,
Planets spin, they call it home.
Gravity pulls with a cheeky grin,
In this fun, we dive right in.

Lightyears leap and hop around,
In this playground, joys abound.
Who knew space could be so fun?
Join the dance, let's all run!

Laughter echoes through the void,
With each quip, we are buoyed.
In this vast and silly blend,
The joy of space, we'll never end.

Humorous Horizons

Beyond the clouds, a jester plays,
Tickling stars in clever ways.
The sun winks with a golden ray,
While planets joke on cosmic days.

Space-time bends, a comical tale,
Black holes giggle, never pale.
Shooting stars leave trails of cheer,
Whispering jokes for all to hear.

The Milky Way, a swirling jest,
With every twist, it feels like rest.
In the cosmos, laughter grows,
As mirth, like stardust, freely flows.

Falling meteors, dressed in light,
Seem to trip in sheer delight.
Every orbit, every spin,
In this vast play, we all win!

Amusing Astronomical Adventures

On cosmic rides through skies so wide,
We tickle meteors that glide.
Saturn's rings, a funny sight,
Like hula hoops in joyous flight.

Jovian storms laugh out loud,
A raucous rumble, a wild crowd.
Each planet spins its merry tune,
Beneath the watchful, giggly moon.

Uranus jokes with a spin so sly,
As Neptune winks a twinkling eye.
Voyager sails with zest and glee,
Charting laughs throughout the spree.

A comet's tail trails out its cheer,
Bouncing through the atmosphere.
In this adventurous space we roam,
Laughter's light will guide us home.

Moonlit Merriment

Under the moon, the shadows play,
Whispering jokes till break of day.
Crickets laugh in harmony,
While stars share secrets joyfully.

Lunar beams throw playful sights,
In this realm of laughing nights.
The night-wind hums a silly tune,
As craters dance beneath the moon.

With each chuckle from afar,
The darkened skies feel like a bar.
Cosmic jokes, we share, we cheer,
In this mirthful atmosphere.

Clouds drift by with playful sighs,
Mirroring the twinkling skies.
In moonlit joy, we lift our hearts,
In this theater, laughter starts.

Lighthearted Exploration

Beneath the stars, a silly dance,
We twirl and spin, not leaving a chance.
Galaxies giggle in cosmic delight,
As comets throw pies in the quiet night.

Jupiter's moons play hide and seek,
While Saturn's rings jingle with a creak.
Asteroids chuckle in playful flight,
Creating laughter in the vast starlight.

Tales of Tickle

In a galaxy filled with quirky sights,
Space critters share their wild delight.
A star sneezed, causing a cosmic quake,
Planets rolled over, all wide awake.

Nebulae whisper silly lines,
As meteors laugh, donning goofy signs.
Each twinkling star winks with glee,
In this jolly place, we're all carefree.

Nebular Nonsense

Floating on clouds of cotton candy,
Galactic giggles feel so dandy.
Black holes swallow laughter whole,
Leaving trails of joy, that's their goal.

Silly planets spin in circles wide,
With cheeky moons dancing side by side.
Their playful pranks, a sight to behold,
In this wacky place, stories unfold.

The Milky Way Misadventure

Come join the fun in cosmic realms,
Where laughter reigns and joy overwhelms.
Stars tell tales that twist and turn,
In this bright void, we laugh and yearn.

Spaceships with smiles zoom through the night,
Chasing stardust, oh what a sight.
With every giggle, we journey far,
On our madcap ride through the stars.

Cosmic Jests

The stars wink down, a playful spark,
Galaxies whirl in a merry arc.
Black holes giggle, pulling us near,
While comets dance, spreading good cheer.

Mars chuckles, its red dust swirls,
Saturn's rings jingle, as laughter unfurls.
Planets in orbit, they trade silly faces,
All in the vastness, joy interlaces.

The moons play pranks on the quiet earth,
Creating chaos, generating mirth.
Stardust tickles the cosmic air,
Bringing giggles from everywhere.

In this grand stage, humor takes flight,
Laughter echoes, from day into night.
A cosmic dance, a jolly parade,
Where jokes are made, and worries fade.

Whispers of Witty Wonder

The sky whispers jokes in a soft, bright tone,
As shooting stars trick each night, alone.
Clouds make faces, fluffy and round,
While sunshine radiates laughter profound.

Nebulas swirl in colors so bright,
Crafting puns out of pure starlight.
Planetary parties, with laughter to share,
Each orbit spins tales of fun in the air.

Asteroids giggle as they zip by fast,
With playfully wild stories from the past.
Galactic giggles spread wide like a beam,
In this vast cosmos, we all share the dream.

Witty wonders flutter like butterflies,
In the expanse, where the funniest lies.
This playful ballet of stars, oh so chic,
Brings laughter to light, leaving us all mystique.

Celestial Quips

In the night sky, a joke takes flight,
As planets chuckle, twinkling so bright.
Venus teases with her dazzling grin,
While Jupiter laughs, letting mirth spin.

Supernovae burst in glee and delight,
Spreading quips in the dark of night.
Constellations share tales from afar,
Each star a witness to humor bizarre.

Galaxies collide, in a frolicsome dance,
Creating a ruckus, a comic chance.
Astro-antics ripple throughout space,
With comets zipping, a wondrous race.

Every whisper from the cosmic seas,
Bursts of laughter carried on the breeze.
Join the parade of celestial cheer,
For humor's the treasure that draws us near.

Astral Amusements

From the depths of space, a giggle is heard,
As starlit comedians whip out a word.
Neptune bubbles, with its watery joke,
While Mercury dashes, quick as a poke.

Lunar laugh tracks echo through time,
Creating ballets in cosmic rhyme.
Pulsars blink, sending cheeky cues,
As asteroids chuckle in stellar hues.

Gravity pulls us into the fun,
Where space emits laughter, never to shun.
The orbits align, each star partakes,
In a laughter-filled dance, for joy's own sake.

Astral amusements, floating so high,
Across the cosmos, where whimsies fly.
Every twinkle, a jest from the sky,
In this merry expanse, we endlessly sigh.

The Celestial Chuckle

Stars twinkle with glee,
As planets spin in jest.
A comet cracks a smile,
While meteors jest at rest.

Galaxies burst with laughter,
Their spirals swirl and twist.
Even black holes giggle,
In a cosmic funny list.

Asteroids dance in moonlight,
With quips that paint the night.
A supernova snickers,
In its brilliant, bright flight.

In this vast, wacky space,
Joy travels light years fast.
When laughter fills the void,
You know the fun will last.

Intergalactic Intuition

Aliens share a chuckle,
With coffee brewed from stars.
They swap their silly stories,
And take a ride on Mars.

Warp-speed humor's flowing,
Like light-years through the night.
Each joke's a cosmic wonder,
Bringing worlds pure delight.

Planets play hide and seek,
While asteroids roll in mirth.
In this galactical game,
Laughter's the greatest worth.

Quirky quarks are giggling,
In every atom's cheer.
Science meets divinity,
When joy's the pioneer.

Stars of Satire

Shooting stars are pranksters,
Darts of light that tease.
Venus winks to Saturn,
"Your rings are just a breeze!"

Jupiter's big laughter,
Rumbles out of sync.
While Mars paints silly faces,
In cosmic orange ink.

Comets tell the best tales,
They take the stage with flair.
In the vastness of the night,
Humor's everywhere!

With every twinkling jest,
The cosmos holds its youth.
In this realm of banter,
We find the joy of truth.

The Comedic Celestial Sphere

Orbiting around laughter,
Are moons that spin and sway.
If you listen closely,
You'll hear them laugh and play.

Stars burst with silly light,
As constellations grin.
Every twirl in space,
Is a dance that has no end.

Nebulas bloom with joy,
In colors bright and bold.
Their giggles echo softly,
In patterns brave and old.

So float among the comets,
In this stellar array.
A joke transcends the cosmos,
In the silliest of ways.

Whimsical Wanderings

In a land where socks just roam,
A hat finds comfort far from home.
The moonplays tricks with jolly grace,
While stars chuckle in their space.

A bear in shades does disco moves,
As crafty crickets play their grooves.
Pineapples dance with twinkling glee,
And all the trees hum sweet melody.

Balloons dive deep into the cake,
While jellybeans take a nice long break.
The sun beams down with goofy flair,
And lollipops twirl in the air.

A flock of ducks in party hats,
Strut like kings, proud with their chats.
It's a silly world, so full of cheer,
Where laughter echoes year by year.

Laughter Across the Void

A comet sneezes, and stars collide,
While aliens giggle in their ride.
In this realm where chuckles bloom,
A black hole swirls with a joyous tune.

Planets hop, and moons conspire,
To launch a joke—a cosmic choir.
Wormholes twist with laughter's grace,
Tickling time in this wild space.

Space cats pounce on floating pies,
As meteorites wink with surprise.
Vacuum laughs as asteroids play,
In a galaxy bright where jesters sway.

With every quasar's gleeful gleam,
And light years wrapped in a funny dream,
We traverse moments, afar and near,
In giggles echoing through the sphere.

Galactic Giggles

In constellations, pranks unfold,
With starry jokes that never get old.
A nebula shimmers with playful light,
As asteroids tumble, a comical sight.

Eclipses hide and seek in time,
While planets spin to a silly rhyme.
Saturn's rings play tag so bright,
In cosmic parties that last all night.

Frogs in space suits hop around,
In laughter's grip, where joy is found.
Galaxies twirl in playful spins,
And clownish comets chase their whims.

With every tick of the universe's clock,
Gravity grins beneath the rock.
So let's toast to fun, cosmic and grand,
In this merry dance across the land.

Orbiting Jokes

On merry orbits of joy we glide,
Where giggles rise and worries hide.
An asteroid tosses jokes like balls,
Whilst shooting stars lose their mind in thralls.

In the rings of Saturn, laughter swirls,
As cheeky moons share funny pearls.
And friendly suns burst out in glee,
With rays of humor shining free.

Comets waltz with clouds of cream,
In silly spaces, a radiant dream.
The laughter echoes, bright and bold,
In this vast cosmos, forever untold.

So let's spin tales, both quirky and bright,
As we orbit together through the night.
From cosmic depths to heights above,
We share a universe, filled with love.

Hilarity in High Orbit

In a rocket of giggles, we soar so high,
Floating past planets with laughter that fly.
Stars wink and chuckle, they join in the spree,
Dancing on comets, just you and me.

Asteroids shout with a bellyache glee,
Shooting across the sky, wild and free.
Galaxies twist in a humorous spin,
As we share jokes with a cheeky grin.

Nebulas puff with a colorful cheer,
Sprinkling stardust, we disappear.
Gravity pulls us back, but we just can't fall,
In this cosmic circus, we've conquered it all.

Planets play tag, while the moons do a jig,
While we roll on the stardust, laughing so big.
Laughter echoes through the vacuum so bright,
In this joyful expanse, everything feels right.

Tickle the Tides of Time

With a wink of the clock, the tickles commence,
As we ride the waves of time in pure suspense.
Each moment's a giggle, a nifty surprise,
Sailing on seconds with laughter in our eyes.

Past meets the present, where jesters now play,
Pirouetting snapshots from yesterday.
Each tick brings a chuckle, each tock holds a grin,
A dance with the futures where nonsense begins.

Time-traveling jesters with slapstick flair,
Balancing clocks on their heads, without a care.
Bouncing through ages like bubbles on air,
Making echoes of giggles that tickle everywhere.

With every chime, the ripple of glee,
A tapestry of laughter, just you and me.
In the whirl of the moment, we splash and we spin,
Forever entwined in this joyful din.

Celestial Caper

A caper in space with a playful brigade,
Constellations join in the pranks we've laid.
Winking at stardust, slipping on moons,
    Tickling orbits with silly cartoons.

Astro-clowns juggle with rings of bright light,
While aliens cheer from their ships in delight.
Comets take bow, as they zip past in style,
In a meteor shower, we dance and we smile.

Galactic gigglers who mimic the suns,
Chasing their tails while they plot all the funs.
Echoes of chuckles reverberate wide,
As we tumble through space on this joyful ride.

Through cosmic capers, we share our delight,
With laughter so rich, it ignites the night.
Underneath this vast quilt of twinkling gleam,
We cling to the humor, living the dream.

Echoes of Euphoria

When the sun breaks and beams with a smile,
Joyful echoes bounce down the cosmic aisle.
Laughter ripples, a soft serenade,
In the playground of planets, our worries do fade.

Galaxies giggle with radiant flair,
As starlight skips lightly, throwing joy in the air.
Comets are chuckling in their shiny attire,
Weaving through space, setting laughter afire.

Distant horizons hum a light-hearted tune,
While the milky way sways in the glow of the moon.
Every twinkling star serves as our guide,
To a party of echoes where grins cannot hide.

In this vastness of joy, laughter we glean,
Embracing the moments, full of serene.
With a wink and a laugh, we embrace what's near,
In the echoes we cherish, we conquer all fear.

Celestial Comedy

In the sky, a star slips by,
Tripping over clouds so high.
A giggle echoes, bright and loud,
As moonbeams dance, a cheeky crowd.

Comets chase with tails aflame,
Joking planets play their game.
Asteroids roll with wobbly grace,
In this vast, whimsical space.

Galaxies swirl with playful cheer,
Whispers of laughter we all hear.
Stardust sprinkles, a cosmic jest,
In this comedy, we feel blessed.

Shooting stars flash silly signs,
Sending giggles through the lines.
From every corner, joy takes flight,
In this astral, funny night.

Laughter Among the Stars

A planet spins with silly hats,
While moons engage in playful chats.
Saturn's rings tickle nearby,
As laughter bursts from the sky.

Orbits twist in jolly ways,
As stars parade through cosmic rays.
Nebulae wink with vibrant hues,
Sharing secrets, the best kind of news.

Galactic giggles fill the void,
In this realm, all cares destroyed.
Echoes of joy in every breeze,
A serenade among the trees.

Astro-dancers spin and sway,
Crafting smiles to light the way.
In a galaxy of pure delight,
We find humor, shining bright.

Shimmering Smiles

Stars wink down with joy and grace,
Filling the night, a happy place.
Twinkling beams of cheerful light,
Inviting fun in every flight.

Meteor showers, a laugh parade,
Each spark a joke that won't degrade.
With each flash, a story told,
Laughter wrapped in stardust gold.

Cosmic rhythms play the tune,
Of laughter echoing with the moon.
In the vastness, smiles collide,
Sharing humor with galactic pride.

A tapestry of joy awaits,
As the universe celebrates.
In every smile, a shimmer bright,
A cosmic jest in the night.

Nebulae of Humor

In clouds of color, joy resides,
Where giggles chase the cosmic tides.
Nebulae blush in vibrant hues,
Spreading laughter as they diffuse.

Planets joke about their size,
While starlit laughter fills the skies.
Witty comets zoom and glide,
Creating chuckles far and wide.

A bustling cosmos, full of cheer,
Where every blink draws laughter near.
Galactic blunders, a playful sight,
Making the heart feel light and bright.

With each twist and turn of fate,
Astral puns we celebrate.
In the expanse, humor finds its home,
In nebulae where wild jokes roam.

Cosmic Tickles

Stars giggle in the night,
Asteroids dance with delight.
Planets spin in silly grace,
Galaxies wear a smiling face.

Comets swoosh with a chuckle,
Black holes play a friendly shuffle.
Nebulas burst in joyful hues,
Creating laughter in the views.

Space dust tickles the air,
Wormholes laugh without a care.
Aliens share a hearty cheer,
In this vastness far and near.

Cosmic jokes float on the breeze,
Each whimsy crafted with ease.
Lightyears may keep us apart,
Yet laughter lives in every heart.

Beyond the Twilight Merriment

The sun sets with a wink,
Moons giggle, don't you think?
Stars play peekaboo at night,
While space critters take flight.

Galactic giggles softly ring,
As meteors leap and spring.
In shadowy realms, we find,
Joy that tickles the mind.

Eclipses play hide and seek,
Leaving us with rosy cheeks.
Stardust dances, swirls in flight,
Wearing smiles both day and night.

Beyond twilight, laughter flows,
As the universe brightly glows.
Every twinkle tells a tale,
Of joy that will never fail.

Gravitational Guffaws

For every force that pulls us near,
There's a joke that we can hear.
Gravity, in its playful way,
Tricks us all on a merry day.

Planets roll in joyous spins,
While Saturn's rings invite the grins.
Asteroids laugh and shoot by fast,
Creating mirth that's meant to last.

Stars fall down like jokes from space,
Landing in a silly place.
In cosmic games, we all partake,
Sharing chuckles with each quake.

With each orbit and bright ray,
Laughter guides us on our way.
In this dance of the night sky,
We find humor that can't deny.

The Humor of Planets

Mars tells jokes in red delight,
While Venus giggles, oh so bright.
Jupiter laughs with its great storms,
Creating whims that take new forms.

Neptune splashes with a grin,
As Saturn's rings begin to spin.
Earth winks, creating a scene,
Of playful antics in the green.

Uranus hides and snickers low,
Sharing secrets only stars know.
In orbits, laughter fills the void,
A joyful sound that can't be destroyed.

Each planet makes a different sound,
With humor spread all around.
In this cosmos vast and wide,
Fun and laughter always abide.

Galactic Guffaws

Stars collide in giggled light,
Planets spin with sheer delight.
Nebulas burst in colors bright,
Laughter echoes through the night.

Aliens dance on Martian ground,
With silly songs, they sing around.
Comets zoom in crazy styles,
Jokes explode like shooting miles.

In black holes, chuckles whirl,
Asteroids share a twinkling swirl.
Gravity pulls with joyful might,
Making joy take off in flight.

A cosmic joke, a playful tease,
Tickling moons with a gentle breeze.
In this vast dance of mirth and cheer,
The universe spins, with laughter near.

Moonbeam Mischief

Under the glow of a playful moon,
Bunnies hop in a comic tune.
With cheese and giggles, they convene,
A banquet fit for a silly scene.

Crickets hum a jazzy beat,
While shadows dance on tiny feet.
Stars wink brightly, sharing glee,
A nighttime party, wild and free.

In the sky, a comet slides,
Spreading smiles to all it rides.
Moons flip flop in cosmic grace,
As laughter fills the outer space.

With mischievous glints in their eyes,
Creatures gather, no sad goodbyes.
In this realm where giggles bloom,
Joy expands and fills the room.

The Cheerful Constellation

Orion tickles with a starry hand,
While Sirius plays in a junk food band.
Together they weave a story bright,
A tapestry spun from pure delight.

Little stars poke fun at the moon,
Juggling comets, a playful tune.
With each flicker, a smile is cast,
In this cosmic jest, joy holds fast.

Galaxies twirl in silly spins,
Each twinkling light invokes vast grins.
A humor comet darts here and there,
Waving joy in the buzzing air.

In this cheerful cosmic dance,
Each light shares a playful chance.
Together they paint the velvet sky,
With laughter that can make you fly.

Spaced-Out Smiles

Floating in zero-gravity fun,
Satellites race, oh what a run!
With every twist, they giggle loud,
Creating mischief in a starry crowd.

Asteroids tickle as they roll,
Moon craters hide a laughing soul.
Black holes swirl with a twinkling wink,
Drawing in giggles, as stars all sink.

Cosmic jokes spin through the void,
Punchlines made for each kind of joy.
Every nova shines a bright grin,
Crafting hilarity from within.

With a flip and twist, the cosmos gleams,
As laughter dances in light-filled beams.
In this vastness, smiles grow wide,
Spaced-out joy, all laughter's pride.

The Humor of the Heavens

In galaxies wide, jokes do abide,
Where comets zoom past with silly pride.
Planets spin round in a dance so bright,
While meteorites laugh in their flight.

A quasar chuckles, shining its light,
Winking at moons during the night.
Asteroids tumble, finding their groove,
In the cosmic ballet, they prove their move.

Shooting stars wink, making wishes fly,
While Saturn's rings wave hello to the sky.
Einstein's grin is near black holes' tease,
Caught in the whirl, one can't help but please.

From the Milky Way's crests to voids so deep,
The laughter of space is a gem to keep.
With every twinkle, a giggle's found,
In the joyful hum of the starry sound.

Constellation Capers

In the big dipper, a prankster swirls,
A juggler of stars, creating pearls.
Orion's belt, with tales to spin,
Of playful brawls where the fun begins.

Playful Ursa mimes a bear's move,
As playful children in night's groove.
Cassiopeia grins, a queen on her throne,
Telling stories of laughs, fetching and grown.

Perseus trips on his mighty sword,
While Andromeda rolls, never bored.
Each twinkling point, a comedian's spark,
Lighting the heavens, leaving its mark.

Their antics weave through the night so grand,
Constellations dancing, hand in hand.
In the skies above, a playful jest,
In every flicker, they mirror our best.

Laughter in the Ether

Beyond the stratosphere where echoes play,
Silly voices bounce, in a bubble array.
Uranus giggles at Neptune's frown,
While Jupiter spins, wearing his crown.

The sun beams brightly, a jester in gold,
With solar flares that never grow old.
Venus whispers secrets, soft and small,
To restless comets that dash and sprawl.

Galaxies swirl in a comedic dance,
Each twinkling light gives laughter a chance.
Echoes of mirth spread over the night,
Filling the vastness with pure delight.

Cosmic charades travel light-years afar,
With jokes that stretch from the Earth to a star.
In the silent vacuum, joy finds its way,
Where laughter in ether forever will play.

Stars of Tickling

In the night sky, a tickling spree,
Stars dance in glee, oh so carefree.
A wink here, a glow there, what a sight,
As comets play tag in the shimmering light.

A star sneezes sparkles, what a surprise!
While planets erupt in hearty cries.
Laughter rings out from the depths of space,
As black holes giggle, hiding their face.

Nova laughter bursts, a firework show,
Each flash a chuckle, in cosmic flow.
Echoes of joy, drifting from afar,
In the tinkling silence of evening's bazaar.

With every blink, a new comic tale,
Across the abyss where laughter prevails.
The night sky's canvas, painted with pride,
Shows a ticklish world where chuckles reside.

Endless Enthusiasm

In a world where giggles fly,
Joyful whispers dance on high,
Bouncing clouds with playful grace,
Tickling stars in cosmic space.

Silly hats and dazzling fun,
Prancing under the bright sun,
Wobbly walks and clownish pranks,
Laughter echoing in sweet banks.

Every quirk like a comet bright,
Chasing shadows, holding tight,
Jesters leap in frolicsome play,
Turning moments into bright sway.

With each chuckle, spirits soar,
A chorus of joy forever more,
In this realm where smiles ignite,
The spark of humor feels just right.

Laughter Through the Galaxies

Across the night, the giggles fly,
Witty twinkles in the sky,
Player stars in a cosmic game,
Laughter echoing, never the same.

Shooting jokes like meteors bright,
Chasing darkness, filling the night,
Galactically quirky, wild, and free,
Between the planets, pure jubilee.

In a swirl of joy, the comets tease,
Bubbling mirth that aims to please,
Stars align for the punchline's cheer,
Orbiting humor, crystal clear.

Nebulae shimmer with laughter tones,
Asteroids tickle, playful stones,
In this vastness, a joyful dance,
Every moment a chance for a chance.

Comedic Cosmos

Planets spin with goofy grins,
Whirling in their cheeky sins,
Orbiting laughter, a bright delight,
In the cosmic waltz, spirits take flight.

Quirky figures on merry trails,
Through the stardust, laughter sails,
With each burst of humor bold,
Tales of giggles waiting to be told.

Astrological puns in swell,
Jovial vibes like a joyful bell,
Galaxies mingle in amusing rounds,
A ballet of laughter, joy abounds.

Witty wonders twirl and sing,
Dancing to the joy they bring,
In this space of endless cheer,
Every chuckle brings us near.

Gravity's Gag

Falling laughter, what a sight,
Gravity stretching to the light,
Wobbly moves in zero G,
Tripping over hilarity.

With every leap, a giggle bursts,
Space-time bending in frolic first,
Weightless wisecracks fill the air,
Floating jokes without a care.

Silly strings tie laughter tight,
Cosmic puppets dancing bright,
Gravity's pull can't bring us down,
We wear the universe like a crown.

In this realm of endless jest,
Funny constellations, we are blessed,
With smiles orbiting every star,
The joy of comedy, near and far.

Playful Planets

In the sky, they spin and twirl,
Around the sun, they swirl and swirl.
Mars tells jokes with a rusted grin,
While Saturn chuckles with its ringy spin.

Venus dances, bright and bold,
Spinning tales, both new and old.
Mercury zips, with a wink and a nod,
While Earth chuckles, a merry little clod.

Jupiter boasts of its great big storm,
But in its heart, it keeps warm.
Nebulas giggle in cosmic delight,
As the stars chuckle through the night.

Each planet plays its silly game,
Eager to share a joke or a name.
In this vast space where laughter flows,
Celestial comedy always grows.

The Jovian Jest

In the shadows of moons, a jest is spun,
Jupiter grins, always on the run.
With swirling storms and colors galore,
It laughs so hard, it shakes to the core.

Tiny moons echo with joyous shouts,
Rolling around with no hints of doubts.
Galileo chuckles at what he once saw,
A dance of gas that leaves none in awe.

The Great Red Spot knows a prank or two,
As it winks at the Sun and says, "Howdy-do!"
Spinning in circles, it plays hide and seek,
With the twinkling stars, a game so unique.

Every storm cloud bursts with giggles loud,
While the asteroid belts form a chuckling crowd.
Beyond the rings, where space is vast,
Laughter ties the cosmos, forever to last.

Rocketing Laughter

Blast off into the cosmic skies,
With rockets that tickle and giggle, oh my!
Engines roar with a comical tune,
As astronauts dance under the light of the moon.

In zero G, they float and they glide,
With rubber chickens on every side.
Each mission starts with a pun-filled cheer,
Making the stars bend down to hear.

Mars explorers play catch with dust,
Turning serious work into absolute must.
From launch to landing, the humor ignites,
Building connections through laughter-filled nights.

Galactic adventures with slapstick flair,
Rocketing joy, floating in air.
In the vast unknown, where dreams take flight,
The cosmos echoes with delight and bright.

Supernova Smiles

When stars explode, they burst in laughs,
Creating sparkles, with cosmic gaffes.
Each supernova, a glittering spree,
Lighting up galaxies, wild and free.

They pop like popcorn, so loud and bright,
Filling the void with gleeful light.
Planets chuckle at the glowing show,
Watching the grainy, glowing confetti blow.

Clusters giggle as they collide,
In this great dance, nothing to hide.
A universe teems with lighthearted cheer,
As comets zoom past and volunteer.

From the tiniest quark to the grandest star,
The laughter echoes, no matter how far.
In the realm of space, where shadows play,
The joy of creation will always stay.

Lightyear Laughs

In a rocket made of cheese,
The cows moo in the breeze.
They dance in zero gravity,
Twirling in hilarity.

With space donuts flying high,
A donut hole for a pie.
Astro-ants wear tiny hats,
Joking with the space bats.

Neon stars play hide and seek,
While comets sing and squeak.
The aliens, in their bright suits,
Trade their jokes like funny boots.

Laughing echoes through the void,
In every heart, joy's deployed.
With giggles floating far and wide,
In this cosmic, funny ride.

Asteroid Antics

Asteroids bounce like rubber balls,
While space mice play in the halls.
A cactus on a comet sings,
Telling tales of silly things.

Galaxy gremlins throw a feast,
Where everyone's a laughing beast.
Pizzas spin with pepperoni,
In a style so macaroni!

Space whales dip and dive in glee,
Flinging water with jubilee.
They shower stars with sparkly seas,
As planets giggle with the breeze.

With every laugh, a world pops,
Creating joy that never stops.
From the sun to distant shores,
Laughter lights in cosmic roars.

Jovial Journeys

Take a ride on giddy beams,
Where rockets burst with laughter themes.
Planets spinning, all aglow,
With funny faces in a row.

Jester moons with painted grins,
Crack the jokes, and everyone wins.
Dancing stars in twinkly shoes,
Join in fun, there's no excuse!

Nebulae play hopscotch through space,
While meteorites join the race.
Their chuckles blend with cosmic winds,
As joy in every corner spins.

So pack your bags for light leaps,
With belly laughs that run so deep.
In this dance of whimsy and fun,
The journey's only just begun.

Celestial Chuckles

Oh, the moons, they laugh so loud,
Beneath a starry, giggly crowd.
Glittering stars tell silly tales,
Of wacky space-time wails.

A pink squid in a space suit leaps,
While cosmic kittens make some heaps.
They juggle planets made of cheese,
While laughing hapless space bees.

Comets trailing sparkly dust,
Join the fun, it's a must!
With every burst of laughter bright,
Galaxies shimmer in delight.

Here the universe knows no frowns,
Just joyous giggles in cosmic towns.
With every chuckle ringing clear,
A harmonious dance, we hold dear.

Cosmic Giggles

In a void, where silence dwells,
Planets spin with secret swells.
Comets grin as they pass by,
Winking suns in the clear sky.

Asteroids dance, they trip and twirl,
They tease the moons, give them a whirl.
Nebulas puff and snicker bright,
Stardust chuckles in the night.

Galaxies twinkle, a lovely sight,
With humor vast, they take flight.
Black holes giggle, pulling all in,
What a place for laughter to begin!

So soar on waves of joy and cheer,
In this space, there's nothing to fear.
For every star that's shining high,
Holds a jest underneath the sky.

Stars that Chuckle

In the night, the stars convene,
Whispering jokes, bright and keen.
Each one shines with a funny tale,
Light years away, they laugh and sail.

Planets burst with glee so bold,
Funny stories of ancient gold.
Jupiter's belly, it quakes with mirth,
While Saturn spins rings of worth.

A comet shoots, a slippery slide,
Through the cosmos, joy will ride.
Orbits twist into giggling loops,
Let's join the fun with all the troops.

When space is quiet, joy will bloom,
In the echoes of the cosmic room.
So gaze above, let your heart free,
For every star beams "Laugh with me!"

Celestial Whimsy

Among the stars, so bright and bold,
Lies a tale that's often told.
Asteroids play hide and seek,
While solar flares play peek-a-boo sneak.

Planets spin with dizzy flair,
Giggles waft in the cool night air.
Meteor showers, a comedy show,
With each bright flash, delight will flow.

The universe wears a jester's cap,
With planets giggling, caught in a trap.
Laughter echoes through the void,
Making even the astroids overjoyed.

So chart a course through laughter's song,
In the night, where we all belong.
For in this space, joy's the key,
Unlocking smiles for you and me.

Laughter Across the Cosmos

In the dark, where starlight beams,
Galaxies spin with funny dreams.
Constellations map a silly game,
With every twinkle, it's never the same.

The moon raises an eyebrow sly,
As comets rush, and planets fly.
Distant worlds share a knowing grin,
Together, they dance in perfect spin.

A supernova bursts with glee,
Filling the void with jubilee.
Laughter ripples through time and space,
Bringing joy to the cosmic place.

So float on whims, let humor roam,
In the vastness, we find our home.
For laughter's light, like stars, persists,
In this grand show, we all exist.

Gravity's Giggling Grip

In a world where toes can fly,
And jellybeans bounce in the sky.
The moon cracks jokes, not too shy,
While comets zoom and wink goodbye.

Stars chuckle softly, twinkling bright,
Each flicker is pure delight.
Cosmic clowns, what a sight,
Spinning tales in the velvet night.

Planets play tag, so carefree,
Asteroids dance with glee.
A big, round sun shines on me,
Laughter echoes endlessly.

In the darkness where they swirl,
Giggles give the void a twirl.
Every shadow, every whirl,
Turns sober space to a joyful pearl.

Whimsical Winks from the Void

A galaxy of silly dreams,
Where stardust flows like bubbling streams.
Planets wear their wackiest beams,
And rockets burst with laughter's themes.

Black holes tickle stars so bright,
They giggle softly, pure delight.
Nebulas blush in colorful light,
In the vastness, all feels right.

Dancing quarks in a merry spree,
Mirth in the atoms, wild and free.
Cosmic jokes in harmony,
In every particle, glee's decree.

Each twinkling star plays peekaboo,
With every race, it's never blue.
Laughter in waves, forever true,
Whispers of joy shared by a few.

Jovian Jests

On swirling storms, the giants play,
With colorful bands that swirl and sway.
Their laughter echoes, bold and gay,
As lightning zings in a bright ballet.

Moons giggle as they spin in glee,
Chasing shadows, wild and free.
In jovial jest, they bounce with glee,
What a play in this cosmic sea!

Around the rings, the merriment flows,
With each twirl, their joy just grows.
Gas giants wink in funny prose,
While laughter thunders, who knows?

They jive and jostle through the void,
Jokes and chuckles, passion deployed.
Spinning tales that can't be destroyed,
In the dance where every soul's buoyed.

Rib-Tickling Realms

In magical lands where giggles roam,
Every planet feels like home.
With merry winds that twist and comb,
Radiant joy is on the dome.

Galactic critters tell their tales,
With cosmic cats leaving trails.
Interstellar ships with wind-filled sails,
Ride on laughter, never fails.

A comet slides with a silly grin,
Laughing as it tumbles in.
With all these smiles, who needs a win?
Every chuckle breaks the din.

So here's to realms where fun runs deep,
Where every star has secrets to keep.
In the universe's joyful sweep,
Whispers of laughter lingers, steep.

Comet's Comedic Tale

A comet zipped by, so spry and bright,
With a wink and a giggle, a fanciful sight.
It danced through the stars, spreading joy like a spark,
Creating a ruckus in the celestial park.

It juggled each planet, a sight to behold,
While asteroids laughed, their humor quite bold.
"Hey, watch this!" it shouted, a tail all aflame,
As it tumbled and twirled, in the galactic game.

Bouncing off moons with a chuckle so grand,
The universe echoed, a joke well-planned.
Each twinkle a punchline, each orbit a jest,
Turning stardust to laughter, it felt like a fest.

And when it took off, leaving behind its glee,
The cosmos erupted, "How funny is he!"
So here's to the comet, with its humor unfurled,
Making us giggle in this vast, wondrous world.

Radiant Revelry

In the radiant glow of the starry night,
Where laughter ricochets with pure delight.
Planets groove like dancers in cosmic ballet,
As the sun cracks a joke to brighten the day.

With meteors zipping, they share a quick jest,
Each burst of bright laughter, a test of the best.
Comets with high spirits race through the void,
While shooting stars giggle, their joy can't be coyed.

Galaxies twirl in whimsical spins,
While cosmic rays tickle the laughter within.
Nebulas chuckle, with hues of surprise,
As the universe beams with giggles that rise.

So let's toast to the stars and their gleeful play,
For in this grand dance, we find our own way.
To revel in joy and embrace the silliness,
In the radiant sky, where we find our bliss.

The Laughing Cosmos

In the laughing cosmos where wonders unite,
Stars share their tales, igniting the night.
Meteorites slapstick with their silly falls,
While black holes snicker, "We'll swallow it all!"

Each galaxy whispers a joke that they spin,
With stardust and giggles that bubble within.
Satellites dance like kids at a show,
Spinning and twirling, with laughter in tow.

Given the chance, the planets would prank,
Swapping their orbits, their comedy rank.
In the swirls of the void, where humor resides,
Every twinkle a chuckle, as joy always glides.

As the universe chuckles with shimmering mirth,
We find in its embrace the warmth of this earth.
So let's laugh with the stars, in their cosmic surprise,
For in the grand scheme, joy never denies.

Joys from the Milky Way

Through the Milky Way's arms, joy frolics and plays,
Stars burst out laughing in rhythm and sways.
Nebulas sparkle with colors so bright,
As chaos and chuckles fill up the night.

With comets as jesters, they dash with flair,
While planets trade stories of humorous air.
The moon shares a giggle with the twinkling sun,
In the grand comedy, they're having such fun.

Galactic giggles echo across every hue,
As black holes chortle, "Come see what we do!"
Spinning and twisting, they tickle through space,
Creating a mirth that we all can embrace.

So raise up your voices and join in the cheer,
For the joys of the Milky Way fill us with cheer.
In this vast stellar dance, let laughter ignite,
As we share in the whimsy throughout the night.

Cosmic Chuckles

In the vastness where comets play,
Stars wink like they know the way.
Galaxies spin in a joyful dance,
Even black holes give chance a glance.

Asteroids roll with a silly grin,
Tickling the moons like kin.
Planets giggle, each in their turn,
While the sun shines bright with a smirk to burn.

Cosmic rays shoot with glee,
As laughter twinkles, wild and free.
Between the rings of Saturn's charm,
Echoes of joy create the calm.

In this space where humor is real,
Each lightyear traveled, a cosmic meal.
So pack your jokes for the light-speed flight,
Let's embrace the fun in the starlit night.

The Laughter Nebula

In clouds where joy and giggles grow,
The laughter nebula starts to glow.
With every puff, a joke takes flight,
As stars throw puns across the night.

Planets hum a cheerful tune,
Dancing gently beneath the moon.
Meteor showers of silly flair,
Bringing bright smiles everywhere.

Cosmic jesters with sparkling hair,
Bounce on moons without a care.
Their playful banter fills the void,
Where silence once loved to avoid.

In this zone of happy dreams,
Laughter flows like interstellar streams.
Join the fun, don't wait or stall,
In this nebula, we're all enthralled.

Jovial Journeys Through the Stars

Let's embark on a giggly ride,
Through starry realms, where laughs abide.
With every turn, we twist and twirl,
In this cosmic carnival, give it a whirl.

Saturn's rings twinkle with cheer,
Echoing laughter we hold dear.
The Big Dipper winks, a cosmic tease,
Inviting all to laugh with ease.

Shooting stars burst with jokes untold,
In a blanket of space, bright and bold.
Traveling far on this radiant spree,
Where humor flows fresh like the galaxy.

So grab a friend, let's share delight,
In this journey through the starry night.
For every smile lights up the sky,
In our jovial voyages, we'll surely fly.

Planetary Punchlines

Round and round the planets spin,
Each one ready for a grin.
Mercury's fast, with quips to share,
While Venus winks with a vibrant flair.

Mars cracks jokes, oh so sly,
As the asteroids leap and fly.
Jupiter roars with laughter grand,
While Saturn's rings clap like a band.

Uranus giggles, a cheeky one,
With a quirky vibe that's never done.
Neptune hums a silly tune,
Drawing smiles beneath the moon.

So grab a seat in this cosmic show,
Where punchlines sparkle and laughter flows.
On planetary trails, let's share a laugh,
In this lighthearted cosmic path.

The Humor of Lightyears

In galaxies far, distance does tease,
Stars wink and chuckle, swirling with ease.
Planets spin tales, amusing and bright,
While comets slip by in giggles of light.

Black holes play tricks, a cosmic jest,
Swallowing stardust, never at rest.
Laughter expands, it echoes through space,
Creating a rhythm, a joyful embrace.

Nebulas dance in a colorful haze,
Each puff a punchline, setting ablaze.
Supernovae pop with a burst of cheer,
Exploding in humor, drawing us near.

A cosmic comedy show on display,
Where the universe laughs in its own funny way.

Starlit Serenades of Joy

Under the night, where stars like to play,
Each flicker a giggle, lighting our way.
Like children at play, they twinkle with glee,
Crafting a symphony, just for you and me.

Planets align in a whimsical dance,
Jupiter's grin, oh what a chance!
Saturn's rings spin jokes all around,
In the vastness of night, hilarity's found.

Shooting stars race, they urge us to wish,
One moment of humor, a delightful swish.
In this cosmic brawl, we chuckle and laugh,
Wishing on wishes, our lighthearted path.

A serenade whispers from the Milky Way's heart,
Where laughter and starlight play a fine part.

Comedic Cosmoscape

In this vast expanse, a joke hits the air,
With each twinkling star, a comedic flare.
Galaxies giggle, their arms wide and free,
As laughter expands through infinity's spree.

Quasars quip in light-years of fire,
Spinning punchlines that never tire.
While Saturn's rings ring in with a chime,
Creating a harmony, oh so sublime.

Gravity's pull holds us close, just in time,
As meteors share tales in rhythm and rhyme.
A cosmic joke that never grows old,
Told through the ages, in stardust, retold.

The canvas of space, a laughter-filled sight,
In every dark corner, the jokes feel so right.

Radiant Revelry

In the glow of the cosmos where laughter's a spark,
Stars bounce and play in this vast, merry arc.
Each moonlit moment a gleeful surprise,
Revealing the humor where joy never dies.

Comets pass by with a cheeky little wink,
Leaving trails of laughter, don't you dare blink!
Cosmic confetti spills from the skies,
Tickling our spirits as humor belies.

As planets collide, they chuckle and tease,
Dancing through space with the greatest of ease.
In this radiant revelry, all hearts align,
For laughter is timeless, a well-aged wine.

Together we beam in this playful delight,
Celebrating the cosmos, our spirits take flight.

Cosmic Crack-Ups

In a galaxy far away, they play,
With jokes and puns bright as the day.
Aliens slip on space banana peels,
Creating a roar that echoes like squeals.

Stars wink with laughter, comets delight,
As cosmic clowns dance under starlight.
Nebulas swirl in colorful cheer,
Making the void sound nothing but clear.

Planets spin while giggling with glee,
Jovian moons juggle in a spree.
Astronauts chuckle, floating around,
In zero-gravity joy, they are found.

Black holes swirl, a comedic spin,
Swallowing laughter, it lets you in.
The cosmos hums a silly little tune,
Under the watchful eye of the moon.

Quasar Quirks

Quasars beam with quirky grace,
Sending out laughter at a fast pace.
With jokes so bright, they light the night,
Even black holes chuckle in fright!

Stars wander, playing hide and seek,
Giggles echo through the cosmic creek.
Galaxies tumble, twist and play,
Their mischief brightens up the gray.

Asteroids fling with a silly twist,
Dancing to tunes that none can resist.
Light-years apart, they share a jest,
Cosmic humor puts all hearts to the test.

Through the void, where silence once lay,
Laughter now rules, come join the play.
Quasars crack up with binaries in sight,
Spreading joy like stardust at night.

Delight in the Dark

In the deep of space where shadows abide,
A chuckle emerges, just like a tide.
Comets dress up in sparkly attire,
Igniting the night with gleeful fire.

Whispers of laughter drift on the breeze,
As planets conspire, they giggle with ease.
In the silence of space, joy finds its way,
In laughter, the darkness will always stay!

Moonbeams prance, tickling stars' feet,
Creating a melody, oh what a treat!
Dancing through orbits, a cosmic ballet,
Spinning tales that keep gloom at bay.

The universe roars, a friendly embrace,
In this dark expanse, find your own space.
From the tiniest quirk to the grandest spark,
There's pure delight in the deep, dark park.

Starship Shenanigans

On a starship soaring through the night,
Crew members giggle at their silly plight.
With mismatched socks and hats askew,
They float in bubbles, joining the view.

Navigating with laughter, it's quite a sight,
Warp speeds buzzing with joy and delight.
Spacesuits dance, and thrusters hum,
As jokes fly faster than they can come.

Asteroid mining for giggles and grins,
Collecting smiles like precious gems.
While engines sputter with comic flair,
Starships roam, banishing care.

Through the cosmos, they share their cheer,
Fueled by laughter, nothing to fear.
Each journey a riot, each meeting a blast,
On starship shenanigans, good times last!

www.ingramcontent.com/pod-product-compliance
Lightning Source LLC
Chambersburg PA
CBHW051648160426
43209CB00004B/831